FRAMEWORK PROFESSIONAL DEVELOPMENT:

Self-study Modules for Teachers and Lecturers

DEVELOP YOUR CLASSROOM MANAGEMENT SKILLS

Roger Smith

Framework Press Educational Publishers Ltd.
Parkfield
Greaves Road
LANCASTER
LA1 4TZ

First published 1995

ISBN 185008 130 1

FRAMEWORK PROFESSIONAL DEVELOPMENT:
Self-study Modules for Teachers and Lecturers
DEVELOP YOUR CLASSROOM MANAGEMENT SKILLS

A catalogue record for the book is available from the British Library

All right reserved

Typeset by Tradespools Ltd., Frome

Printed in Great Britain
by The Charlesworth Group, Huddersfield

Cover design by John Angus
Illustrations by John Fuller

Table of Contents

The Author:

Roger Smith has worked in schools, a college of Further Education, the Open University and the University of Warwick. He has published widely and broadcast on BBC Radio. Seven photocopiable packs have been published by Framework Press: *The Effective School, Volume 1: Teachers Working Together: The Whole School Approach* (1990); *The Effective School, Volume 2: Classroom Techniques and Management* (1990); *The Heads' and Deputies' Handbook: Managing Schools in the 1990s* (1992); *Managing Pupil Behaviour in School and Classroom: In-house Training Materials for Teachers* (1993); *Preparing for Appraisal: Self-evaluation for Teachers in Primary and Secondary Schools* (1993); *Preparing for Inspection: The Whole School Approach* (1994) and *Managing Your Classroom: A Guide to Better Teaching* (1994). As the Headteacher of a large Combined School, he has been involved in INSET committees, whole school development plan committees and the steering and planning groups of several residential summer schools and a national conference. As well as working in school, he teaches undergraduate students at the University of Warwick.

Editor:

Karen Westall

Acknowledgements:

The author would like to thank the many people who have contributed directly and indirectly to the thinking that had culminated in this book:

— all those course and conference members who have helped, often without knowing, to shape the ideas expressed here;

— the staff of Milverton Combined School and many other Warwickshire teachers;

— my wife and children, for their patience;

— Chris Reeve and Elaine Brown who first fired my imagination.

Introduction

Managing and controlling all that happens inside the classroom is perhaps the key issue for all teachers. How successfully a teacher can do this will influence the effectiveness of the teaching and learning that can and does take place.

It has been a commonly held view in the teaching profession that the group management skills necessary in the classroom are natural gifts that you either do or do not possess. This may be true of a small minority, but it is damaging to many teachers who are experiencing crises of confidence and are laying the blame on their own inadequacies, rather than on the lack of particular skills, many of which can be learned through INSET, discussions with colleagues and individual learning.

This book is the first of a series on classroom management, teaching skills and managing pupil behaviour. It is designed for you to work through on your own and to take decisions about your own learning need. As you work through the various Activities, you should become more aware of the teaching styles, skills and techniques that really work for you, while at the same time you should recognise those that you need to improve, possibly with help from others. The final Activity contains a series of Action Plans which concentrate on those areas.

This is a very important process because, as we all know, teachers are more likely to have well-managed classrooms if they are skilled at providing purposeful and stimulating learning experiences to all their pupils by using a variety of delivery methods and styles.

Enjoy the book, read each Activity carefully and be honest. It is the only way to learn. When an Activity asks you to think of something that has happened to you, please do just that. We all learn from our own mistakes and the best teachers reflect on their own practice all the time and learn from their experiences.

Effective and Ineffective Teaching

Let's start with the six basic principles used, either consciously or unconsciously, by all effective teachers. Here they are:

✤ MODEL the attitudes and behaviour that you expect from your pupils

✤ Whichever successful teaching style you use and however you manage your classroom you must be CONSISTENT, FIRM and FAIR

✤ Always use teaching and classroom control strategies that involve PRAISE

Always involve praise.

✤ Show all your pupils that you CARE about their work and their lives both inside and outside the school

✤ There will be times when what you are trying to teach in a certain way and what you are asking pupils to do just doesn't seem to work and will have to be changed. This happens all the time to teachers of all ages and with all kinds of experience. Keep trying and above all be FLEXIBLE

✤ All five of these principles are important and need to form the basis of how you teach and how you manage your classroom. Use them well and make sure that you PERSEVERE

Of course, it's all very well knowing that these six principles for effective teaching are appropriate, are useful and should be part of your classroom routines, but do you follow them?

◆ **ACTIVITY 1.1** ◆◆◆

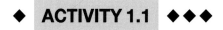

In order to MODEL the attitudes and behaviour that you expect from your pupils, you need to know what kind of behaviour and attitudes you actually want. Only then will you be able to model it. An example of this would be a common, and certainly essential, classroom rule:

Listen carefully when the teacher is talking.

For you to model this expectation would mean that you actually need to listen carefully when pupils are talking to you. In other words, if you want them to listen to you, you must listen to them and, more importantly, your pupils must know that you are doing this.

Write down five aspects of behaviour or attitudes that you expect in your classroom. This could be done in the form of rules, e.g.

Don't talk when I'm talking, or listen when I am talking to you.

In the space beneath each one, write down how you successfully model the behaviour you expect. If you don't successfully model what you want, write down how you aim to do so in the future, e.g.

Don't run around the classroom.
I always move slowly around the room and never move quickly or bump into anyone without saying sorry.

1.

2.
3.
4.
5.

◆ ACTIVITY 1.2 ◆◆◆

For your pupils to recognise that you are in control and that you mean business, it is essential that you are CONSISTENT, FIRM and FAIR in your treatment of them. They will soon know, and not like it, if some of them are unfairly picked on or unfairly favoured. At the same time, most teachers will recognise the need to vary behavioural expectations for particular pupils who have specific problems.

Use *Box 1* to describe a recent incident or occasion when something happened in your classroom that you treated with consistency, firmness and fairness. Use *Box 2* to describe the opposite. Some of you will discover that you are able to say, with a certain degree of confidence, that you *are* CONSISTENT, FIRM and FAIR. Others might find that this is often not the case. Use *Box 3* in whichever way is appropriate.

Box 1

Describe the incident.
What did you do that tells you that you were CONSISTENT, FIRM and FAIR?

Box 2

Describe the incident.
What did you do, or fail to do that suggests that you were not very CONSISTENT, FIRM or FAIR?

Box 3

If you were CONSISTENT, FIRM and FAIR, what did you do that needs to be remembered so that you can do it again and again when future classroom problems arise?
If you weren't very CONSISTENT, FIRM and FAIR, what do you need to do so that you can be more effective? It might also be useful to note down how your pupils reacted. If they react in this way again, it might be because you are repeating the same mistakes.

◆ **ACTIVITY 1.3** ◆◆◆

When you are trying to create a classroom atmosphere where really high quality teaching and learning experiences take place, you need to PRAISE good behaviour, good work, high standards and appropriate attitudes.

At the same time as you are doing this, you also need to make sure that you don't reward or give undue attention to unacceptable behaviour. This Activity can be completed in one of two ways. Either think back to a lesson you have recently taught and list everything that happened that you praised. At the same time, write down what form the praise took, e.g. a pupil arrived with all her pens and pencils for the first time ever and you said something like: 'That's great, Sarah. I'm glad you have got everything. Well done!' The alternative approach is to think ahead to a lesson you will be teaching and list everything that you would like to be able to praise and how you will actually do it. The same chart can be used for both methods. There are six spaces.

What you praised	*How you praised it*
1.	
2.	
3.	
4.	

5.	
6.	

If you have a strong list of useful ways of praising pupils, you should be in a position to be able to use them as often as necessary. If you found the Activity difficult, it will be useful for you to sit down and write a list of praise phrases or sentences, e.g. 'What a neat piece of work ...', or 'Now you're really making progress ...'. Praise in the classroom raises pupils' self-esteem and must be used as often as possible.

◆ **ACTIVITY 1.4** ◆◆◆

Despite what some pupils' behaviour suggests, most, if not all, recognise that certain teachers CARE more about them than others. All of us, including your pupils, want to be liked. Let them all know that you actually care about what happens to them and that, even when they behave inappropriately, it is their actions that you disapprove of, not them. You must raise your pupils' self-esteem in this way.

An example of this might be where a pupil swears at someone. Your reaction should be one of righteous indignation because of the language: 'Don't ever use that kind of language again. It is disgusting. I don't like it and no one else should be listening to it either ...'.

It should not be a case of demolishing the pupil's character and dignity. After all, you don't yet know why s/he was swearing, so avoid saying things like: 'That kind of language from you doesn't surprise me. You always have been stupid and foul mouthed. I find you disgusting and I expect everyone else does as well ...'.

How do you show your pupils that you care about them? What do you do? What do you say?

Choose three recent examples and write them down paying special attention to what you do and say that can be used on other occasions.

1.
2.
3.

◆ ACTIVITY 1.5 ◆◆◆

The final two principles can be examined together. It is not easy to be FLEXIBLE with some pupils but it is important to try to PERSEVERE so that you gradually win their co-operation.

Think of a pupil who is disaffected and/or disruptive or has some other kind of problem that is affecting what happens in the classroom. Being flexible and persevering means thinking about what you have already tried to do to solve the problem and what you might try in the future.

Write down the problem, what you have already tried and what you intend to try. Think long and hard. It could pay dividends later when a different problem might arise, which could be solved using similar techniques.

The problem:	
What I have tried:	**What I am going to try:**

◆ ACTIVITY 1.6 ◆◆◆

The six basic principles that have been reviewed in the previous Activities should be the umbrella beneath which successful teachers develop and improve the quality of the teaching and learning in their classrooms. In fact good teachers will model the behaviour and attitudes they want, will be consistent, firm and fair, will praise their pupils, care about them and have lots of flexibility and perseverance because they will want to raise pupils' self-esteem and develop a positive, lively and interesting work ethos within the classroom. The success of this approach will depend to a large extent on the teaching style – the teacher's actual handling of the teaching and learning processes.

Read each sentence on the *Teaching Style Chart*, in which the styles do not appear in any order of preference. Fill in the box at the end of each one with the number that indicates your ability to use that style:

     1... You are very good at using this style
     2... You are quite good at this
     3... You use this style sometimes and are average
     4... You are quite poor at using this style
     5... You are bad at this and hardly ever use it

Teaching Style Chart

I plan the lesson so that the work extends and motivates all pupils.	
I arrive in the classroom before the pupils.	
I emphasise praise rather than criticism.	
I include pupils in the planning process so they feel involved in what they are doing.	
I take what the pupil brings to the learning task into account, thus helping me to match the task to the pupil.	
I develop opportunities for framing and solving problems.	
I encourage pupils to work co-operatively in groups.	
I avoid sarcasm and ridicule.	
I set realistic goals and deadlines.	
I insist on positive on-task behaviour.	
I ensure that 'discipline' and 'control' are quiet and firm and are an aid to learning.	
I use skilful questioning to encourage pupils to think and use the knowledge that they already have.	
I match any punishments to the pupil and the 'crime' and I do not use blanket punishments against the whole class.	
I use humour, laughter and smiles to create a positive atmosphere.	
I observe pupils' work in the classroom to help with assessment and the regular monitoring of pupil progress.	
I interact with pupils as they work and use this purposeful intervention to help both in the pupils' work and in building up relationships.	
I frequently use good work by pupils as a model to stimulate other pupils.	
I provide continuous feedback to pupils during the lesson.	

I always make clear to the pupils the criteria by which the work will be assessed.	
I move around the room as part of the monitoring process and don't sit at a desk all the time.	
Pupils do not have to wait in queues for my attention.	

Before going on to the next Activity, quickly look back at this one. Have you been honest with yourself? A large part of learning is knowing what you are, and are not, good at. If you need to change any of your responses, do it now, because this chart will be part of a final Action Plan at the end of the book.

◆ ACTIVITY 1.7 ◆◆◆

Look back at *Activity 1.6* and think positively. For this Activity, you are going to think about the teaching styles that you know you use well and try to say how you know and what effect they have on your pupils.

One of the styles that I know I use well is: 'I frequently use good work by pupils as a model to stimulate other pupils'. I would have given this style a score of 1. I know that I use this style well because I display pupils' work all over the classroom and am constantly telling the rest of the class to look at someone's good work and/or praising someone's work out loud. The pupils realise that it is genuine, because they know that I criticise work that I am sure could be much better and that I praise for effort as well as for excellence.

Choose *three* styles that you know you use well, i.e. for which you have scored 1. Write each down and answer the questions that follow carefully.

Style 1:
How do you know you use this style well?

What effect does using this style well have on your pupils?

Style 2:

How do you know that you use this style well?

What effect does using this style well have on your pupils?

Style 3:

How do you know that you use this style well?

What effect does using this style well have on your pupils?

◆ ACTIVITY 1.8 ◆◆◆

It is also important to look at those areas of your teaching style for which you scored 5 or 4 in *Activity 1.6*. It may mean that you don't use this style, can't use this style or use it badly. One of the areas where I used to be weak is: 'Pupils do not have to wait in queues for my attention'. In my classroom there were often queues of pupils waiting for their work to be marked. Pupils who got bored would mess around and I would have to deal with the problems they caused. One way that I dealt with it was learned from a colleague. Rather than mark finished work at my desk, I would constantly move around the classroom marking and assessing all the time, so that there was never a large amount of completed work to mark all at once.

Choose *three* weak styles from *Activity 1.6*. Write them down and answer the questions that follow. This time you are being asked to think ahead to the kind of advice and INSET you might need.

Style 1:
How do you know that you use this style badly?
What do your pupils do?
What do you think you could do to improve this style?
What INSET would help you to improve this style? Which of your colleagues might be able to help?

Style 2:

How do you know that you use this style badly?

What do your pupils do?

What do you think you could do to improve this style?

What INSET would help you to improve this style? Which of your colleagues might be able to help?

Style 3:

How do you know that you use this style badly?

What do your pupils do?

What do you think you could do to improve this style?

What INSET would help you to improve this style? Which of your colleagues might be able to help?

◆ ACTIVITY 1.9 ◆◆◆

Most competent teachers are able to use all kinds of verbal and non-verbal cues as part of their repertoire of skills and styles. In other words, they use their voice and their bodies to send messages to their pupils. If this is done well, pupils quickly pick up the correct messages and behave, work and learn accordingly. Each one of the following cues or messages should tell your pupils something. Each one should either stop them from doing something, encourage them to carry on, reassure them or warn them that you are aware of what they are doing.

After each one write a number from 1 to 5, where 1 implies that you are very good at this and do it often and 5 implies that you either never use it or are bad at using it. 3, of course, suggests that you use it sometimes. In the space beneath each one write down when you use it and what message it usually gives to your pupils.

Cues and Messages

Shaking my head	
Making eye contact	
Making eye contact and using the pupil's name	
Making eye contact and raising my eyebrows	
Pointing my finger and making eye contact	

Putting my finger on my lip and making eye contact	

Smiling at a pupil	

Nodding at a pupil with eye contact and a smile	

Coughing loudly at the front of the class	

Snapping my fingers	

Walking towards a pupil and saying her/his name	

Standing near a pupil after prolonged eye contact	

Sitting next to a pupil	

Raising my voice after eye contact and using a pupil's name	

◆ ACTIVITY 1.10 ◆◆◆

All you need for this final Activity is a large mirror, preferably full length.

Choose *three* of the cues or messages in *Activity 1.9* that you are good at, i.e. where you gave yourself a score of 1 or 2. Practise what you do and how you do it in the mirror.

Now choose *three* that you either don't use but would like to or are bad at. Practise improving these in the mirror.

Remember that what you say, what your face is doing and how you are moving all have to send the same messages to your pupils.

Many of the messages in *Activity 1.9* can be joined together in all sorts of combinations. You could practise other combinations that you feel will work. *But*, I'll say it again! All the messages have to match. It is no good leaning on a radiator, smiling, nodding your head and telling someone off for swearing. Neither is it any good trying to praise someone with low self-esteem if you are frowning at them, standing over them and raising your voice. To be an effective teacher the style has to be appropriate.

❖

Practising cues and messages.

Classroom Management Skills

It is important to recognise that, as a teacher, you have certain characteristics and certain skills you can use to build your successful classroom management techniques. The first section of this Unit suggests some of those characteristics and asks you to think carefully about what you do that will help your learners to work hard and constructively.

◆ ACTIVITY 2.1 ◆◆◆

Managing a classroom concerns both how you organise the room and how you actually teach. Most successful teachers reflect on what they do in the classroom and how they do it. Developing this reflective, thoughtful approach will enable you to learn from your mistakes and develop what you know has worked well.

When you begin to think about your own classroom management and how you teach specific lessons, it is useful to do this within a structured framework.

These eight headings should help. Read each one and respond to the questions.

1. The BEGINNING of the lesson is very important.
Why is it important?
2. The CONTENT of the lesson has to be matched to the ability of the learners.
Why is this important?
3. Lessons have to be PLANNED and PREPARED well.
Why is this important?

4. QUESTIONS and EXPLANATIONS have to be used as part of the teaching style.

Why are these two techniques important?

5. Successful lessons contain different pupil activities. The TRANSITIONS between these different activities are important.

Why are they important?

6. Classroom management involves discipline and order within the classroom. It is important that pupils BEHAVE well and RESPOND to the work they are doing.

Why is it important that this happens?

7. The relationship between teacher and pupil is important. The teacher's ATTITUDE and MANNER are crucial.

Why is this important?

8. Lessons of whatever kind need to have an effective and appropriate ENDING.

Why is an effective ending important?

◆ **ACTIVITY 2.2** ◆◆◆

This Activity takes the eight headings of *Activity 2.1* a stage further. Under each general heading are more specific points. Read each one, think about some of your recent lessons, reflect on how successful you think they were and decide whether you were *EFFECTIVE (E)* or *INEFFECTIVE (I)*. Write in the appropriate letter against each point.

If you were effective suggest why and what you did to make the lesson a success.

If you think you are ineffective at certain classroom management techniques, suggest what you need to do to improve.

Use the spaces below each one to write down your responses.

Classroom Management Skills

1. *The BEGINNING of the lesson:*

I start the lesson positively with a clear signal.	
My pupils are encouraged to start promptly.	
My pupils know exactly what to do at the beginning of my lessons.	

2. *The appropriateness of the lesson CONTENT:*

The work I set is at the correct level for my pupils.	
I am able to set work that matches individual and group needs.	
My work engages my pupils' attention because it is interesting.	
The work I give my pupils is never too easy and never too hard so that my pupils lose concentration.	

3. *The PLANNING and PREPARATION of lessons:*

I always know what I am doing at each stage of the lesson.	

My lesson plan is part of a larger long-term plan rather than just a one-off time-filler.	
My planning sets out clearly the objectives of the lesson, i.e. what the pupils are expected to learn.	
If I need resources, such as videos or OHPs, I don't leave organising this to the last minute.	
Within my lesson planning are opportunities to assess what my pupils are doing.	

4. *The use of QUESTIONS and EXPLANATIONS:*

I use question and answer sessions as a means of giving and receiving information.	

I ask a variety of questions and make sure that I involve the whole class, rather than the same few people.	
Questions are not just one way from me to the pupil. I encourage pupils to ask questions of me and of each other.	

5. *The TRANSITIONS from one activity to another within a lesson:*

I ensure that transitions between different kinds of activity are smooth and trouble free.	
I make sure that there is no excessive noise or movement between activities.	
I plan the transition and change from one activity to another – they don't just happen without any thought.	

Smooth and trouble-free transitions.

6. *The BEHAVIOUR and RESPONSE of the pupils to the work:*

I am aware of everything that is happening in the classroom.	
I make sure that each individual is aware that I am watching her/him and that I know exactly what s/he is doing.	

I know that moving about the room, standing near pupils and talking to them about their work is important.
I regard having positive rules about work and behaviour as essential.

7. *The ATTITUDE and MANNER of the teacher:*

My relationship with the pupils needs to be appropriate, i.e. not too severe or too permissive.
I am approachable during lessons and in corridors and playgrounds, *but* am never alone in closed rooms.
I set examples of the kind of behaviour that I expect of my pupils.

8. *The ENDING of the lesson:*

I make sure my lessons end properly and decisively without confusion.	
As the lesson draws to a close, I attempt to summarise and review what has been taught and learned.	
I introduce some forward planning by suggesting to the pupils what the next lesson is likely to be about.	

◆ ACTIVITY 2.3 ◆◆◆

Most of your pupils, like learners of all ages, will benefit from being involved in their own learning. In managing your teaching you should allow for the following characteristics. Read each one and write down your responses to the question(s) beneath each one.

1. Pupils should be able to ask questions.

How do you allow this to happen? Why is it important to allow this to happen?

2. Learning is partly about being curious about what is being taught.

How do you encourage your pupils to use their natural curiosity?

3. Learners of all ages probably learn a lot from being told certain things.

How do you make sure that this happens in your classroom?

4. Once certain facts have been learned, however, pupils will need to think carefully and solve problems that are associated with these facts.

How will you make sure that this happens? What problems can you see that are associated with this kind of classroom management?

5. Problem-solving is about having time to think, hypothesise and discuss.

Does this happen in your classroom? How do you ensure that it happens?

◆ ACTIVITY 2.4 ◆◆◆

There is a danger in many classrooms that if a teacher sees her/himself solely as the giver of knowledge, there will be an 'us' and 'them' atmosphere. In a classroom managed in this way, the pupils as learners will be passive and, rather than take any responsibility for their own learning, will see it as something that is given to them. Their participation will be minimal and such an atmosphere will increase the danger of boredom and misbehaviour.

Effective classroom management involves a certain amount of working together co-operatively, both between pupils and pupils and teacher and pupils.

Read each one of the following statements and then answer the questions in the spaces.

1. Pupils learn a great deal from one another.
How do you manage your classroom so that this happens?
2. Being part of a group such as a class, rather than an isolate, is important for every pupil's self-esteem.
How do you make sure that each of your pupils feels part of the teaching group? What do you do if you feel that a pupil is being left out?

3. Co-operative learning and working in groups develop pupils' ability to listen to one another's points of view and to learn to make judgements and to take responsibility.

How do you organise groups? What are the problems you might face?

4. Successful teachers are able to work with the whole class, groups and individuals. Grouping pupils so that they work together and learn is difficult.

How do you create groups in your classroom? What is the most effective way?

◆ ACTIVITY 2.5 ◆◆◆

It is important to think about how you teach, how you work in the classroom, what you do successfully and what you need to improve. *Activities 2.1–2.4* should have suggested various areas of classroom management where you are effective or ineffective. This Activity asks simpler questions requiring a *Yes* or *No* answer. If you answer *Yes*, there is no need for any more consideration. If you answer *No*, you need to think carefully about why you don't do this in your classroom.

The Activity can be completed in one of two ways. Either think of one or two lessons that you have taught recently and tick the *Yes* or *No* column, as appropriate, or take the checklist into one or two of your lessons and find time during the lesson to tick the *Yes* or *No* column.

Evaluating Aspects of Classroom Management

	Yes	No
1. Do your lessons include the following teaching styles: — Individual teaching?		
— Group teaching?		
— Whole class teaching?		
2. Do you plan your time constructively so that you can do all of the following: — Give instructions?		
— Question?		
— Explain?		
— Assess?		
3. Do you plan the pupils' time correctly so that realistic deadlines are set?		
4. Do you give your pupils the chance to respond in ways other than writing?		
5. Do you use appropriate body language when you are praising or disciplining your pupils?		
6. Are you good at giving oral instructions that set the scene and explain tasks?		
7. Do you interact well with your pupils as they are working on the tasks set?		
8. Do you use good work by your pupils as a model to stimulate other pupils?		
9. Do you tell your pupils the criteria you will be using to assess their work?		
10. If you were asked, would you be able to tell a colleague the following: — What your pupils are doing?		

— What they are learning?		
— How it fits into your long-term planning?		
11. Are your classroom routines well planned and easily understood by your pupils?		
12. Are you able to tell a colleague the following: — What you are aiming for in the lesson and what your objectives are?		
— What you are learning from what you are teaching and how you are teaching it?		
— How the experiences of this particular lesson will be used in future practice?		

Your lesson aims and objectives.

◆ ACTIVITY 2.6 ◆◆◆

The final Activity in this Unit can be used to rethink many of your responses to earlier Activities.

You will need a large sheet of paper. On it, draw a plan of your classroom. If you work in several different rooms, draw a plan that suggests the most common arrangement of the furniture. Include in your plan such things as the teacher's desk and chair, pupils' desks and chairs, cupboards, book shelves and the position of the door and windows. Finally, mark at least three positions where you usually stand or sit during your lessons.

In previous Activities, you will have discovered your strengths and weaknesses of classroom management and the strategies you use or don't use.

It may be that your management of lessons is sometimes quite closely related to how you manage the space in which you teach. A simple example would be to consider your ability to teach in groups. This might be obvious, but if your classroom has desks and tables in rows, group work will be very difficult. If the desks or tables are grouped together, teaching your pupils in groups will be easier. A more difficult example would be to look at the transitions between different parts of a lesson. If you want to structure the lesson into four parts, e.g. talking to the whole class, working in groups, working individually and finally back as a whole class, you need to make sure that the furniture and space is used in a way that allows flexible movement. If chairs and tables have to be moved at each stage there will be too much noise and pupil movement.

Finally, let's look at the classroom management strategies that you need to develop. There may be many reasons why you are not particularly effective at a certain method of working. Some of them could be changed by better use of your teaching spaces.

Write down *five* classroom management strategies that you need to develop and beneath each one suggest what you might alter in your classroom that would make it easier to improve this aspect of classroom management.

e.g. I am not very good at moving pupils in and out of the classroom quickly and quietly.
I need to start and end my lessons effectively by insisting that everyone is quiet before they enter or leave the room and making sure that each time I do this there is an orderly line.

1.

2.

3.

4.

5.

UNIT

3

Teacher Behaviour

The interaction between teacher and pupil is a complex one. It is important to make sure that you behave in such a way that learning is made as easy and as fruitful as possible. To do that, you need to make sure that you behave in ways that will be considered in this Unit.

◆ ACTIVITY 3.1 ◆◆◆

Read each of the following and use the space to write down what you actually do that shows colleagues and your pupils that you are behaving in this particular way. At the same time, suggest why it is important to behave in such a way.

1. I understand my pupils as individuals and know how they relate to me and the rest of the class.

2. I create an atmosphere in which every pupil can learn.

3. All groups of pupils have a variety of needs. I behave in a way that satisfies both their social and academic needs.

4. All my pupils leave my lessons with a positive self-image and a sense of achievement.

5. In managing my classroom, I have rules and routines that help everyone to learn.

6. In all my dealings with pupils, I work in a quietly confident way.

7. Whenever I am teaching, I give pupils the impression that I expect them to work hard and obey instructions.

8. In working with pupils, I am able to model the kind of positive, constructive, polite, work-orientated atmosphere that I want in my classroom.

◆ **ACTIVITY 3.2** ◆◆◆

One of the first things to do when meeting a class for the first time is to establish your authority. As a teacher, you have to behave as if you are in charge. You are the authority figure, and all your pupils must know what to expect and how to behave when you are teaching them. This means that you will have to establish rules and routines. Examples might include:

Don't talk when I am talking.
Don't run in the classroom.
Don't touch other people's property.
Treat everyone with respect.

We will look at rules in more detail in *Activity 3.3*. What is important, when you are establishing your authority, is to behave in such a way that your pupils know that you are in charge but are not frightened into submission, ridiculed or reduced to having low self-esteem.

There are five essential ways of behaving when you are teaching. Read each one and in the space provided either say how you actually manage to do this and why it is important or, if you don't feel that you behave in this way, say what you will do in the future and why you think that it is important.

1. I need to behave in such a way that I CHALLENGE my pupils. This will mean making sure that when I am teaching I bring all my pupils to a point where their chances of success are good.
2. All my pupils must feel that they have some control over what they learn, how they learn and the pace at which they learn. In other words, I must make an effort to give them FREEDOM TO MAKE DECISIONS about their learning.

3. When I am establishing my rules and making sure that I am in control, I must encourage RESPECT both for and by the pupils.

4. In establishing rules and routines, they must be firm, reasonable and fair and should CONTROL the teaching and learning that takes place.

5. Whatever it is that I am teaching, all my pupils should experience SUCCESS.

◆ ACTIVITY 3.3 ◆◆◆

If you manage to behave in a way that meets all or most of the criteria in *Activity 3.2*, you should be able to establish classroom routines and rules reasonably effectively. In this Activity there are several common classroom rules listed and additional space for two more of your own.

Read each one. In the first space, write down how you would establish this rule firmly but fairly in your classroom. (Rules don't just establish themselves, they have to be worked at.) In the second space, write down what would happen if either this rule didn't exist, or you didn't impose it.

Hopefully, all the rules will be ones you know and approve of. Use the last spaces for any others that you feel are important.

Classroom Rules

1. Arrive punctually, quietly and purposefully, with everything you need for the lesson.
How would you establish this rule?
What are the consequences of not imposing this rule?

2. Listen carefully to the teacher and to each other.
How would you establish this rule?
What are the consequences of not imposing this rule?

3. Respect and support each other and your teacher.

How would you establish this rule?

What are the consequences of not imposing this rule?

4. Always move around slowly and quietly.

How would you establish this rule?

What are the consequences of not imposing this rule?

5. Follow your teacher's instructions and do not distract each other when you are working.

How would you establish this rule?

What are the consequences of not imposing this rule?

6. Always speak politely to everyone, even if you are feeling bad tempered. Never shout as it is impolite and discourteous.

How would you establish this rule?

What are the consequences of not imposing this rule?

7. If the class or group is asked a question, do not shout out the answer. Wait until you are asked.

How would you establish this rule?

What are the consequences of not imposing this rule?

8. Eating, drinking and chewing are not allowed in the classroom.

How would you establish this rule?

What are the consequences of not imposing this rule?

9. No one is allowed to leave the room without permission.

How would you establish this rule?

What are the consequences of not imposing this rule?

10. Swearing and other provocative comments are forbidden.

How would you establish this rule?

What are the consequences of not imposing this rule?

11.

How would you establish this rule?

What are the consequences of not imposing this rule?

12.
How would you establish this rule?
What are the consequences of not imposing this rule?

To end this Activity, it would be useful to check whether your school has a printed list of rules that apply to all teachers. If it does, check through it carefully and see whether the list in this Activity includes all the rules that you need to impose in your classroom.

❖

No eating or drinking in class.

◆ ▨ ACTIVITY 3.4 ▨ ◆◆◆

If you expect your pupils to obey your classroom rules and work well during your lessons, it is important to make sure that you adopt particular patterns of behaviour.

For each of the questions below, write one of the following:

> O … You behave in this way often
> U … You behave in this way usually
> N … You never behave in this way

Your Patterns of Behaviour

1. Do you set high standards?	
2. Do you apply rules fairly and consistently?	
3. Do you expect to give and receive respect?	
4. Do you treat everyone as an individual?	
5. Do you smile and say hello to everyone?	
6. Do you accept the occasional pupil problem as an inevitable part of growing up?	
7. Do you avoid confrontation?	
8. Do you listen when your pupils are talking to you?	
9. Do you use punishment sparingly?	
10. Do you arrive before the class is due to start?	
11. Do you deal with all misbehaviour?	
12. Do you extend and motivate all pupils?	
13. Do you enjoy yourself?	
14. Do you use your pupils' first names?	
15. Do you put examples of your pupils' work on display?	
16. Do you avoid humiliating your pupils?	

17. Do you avoid over-reacting?	
18. Do you avoid blanket punishments, i.e. punishing the whole class for the bad behaviour of one person?	
19. Do you avoid punishing more often than you praise?	
20. Do you avoid sarcasm?	

◆ **ACTIVITY 3.5** ◆◆◆

How you behave within your classroom will affect whether you are an effective or an ineffective teacher. These two simple, yet honest definitions may well suggest into which category you fall:

> An effective teacher has few discipline problems and gives pupils the opportunity to grow and develop in a variety of ways with a variety of outcomes, within an atmosphere of firm, fair and consistent control. S/he has high expectations of the pupils' work and behaviour.

> An ineffective teacher is unsure about how to behave within the classroom and how to apply consistent rules. S/he creates a narrow, teacher-guided environment, where little tolerance for the individual is encouraged and punishment rather than praise is the norm. There is ample opportunity for on-task working, but there are frequent bouts of off-task behaviour. Expectations may well be lower, and the outcomes of a predictable sameness.

Hopefully you will fall into the EFFECTIVE category. If you see some of the INEFFECTIVE characteristics as part of your 'style', don't be too disheartened. They are in all of us. What we all need to do is recognise our failings and work out strategies for overcoming them.

One thing that is certain is that our behaviour in the classroom has to involve making sure that rules do not get broken but that, if they do, as little disruption as possible occurs.

Being firm, fair and consistent does not mean behaving in such a way that pupils get away with causing problems and disrupting your classes.

Effective teachers stop pupils from breaking rules and from behaving badly by operating a system of sanctions. They can range from a minor telling off to reporting a culprit to another teacher, Head of Department, Deputy Head or Headteacher.

Write down some of the sanctions that you use in your classroom.

1. e.g. I keep pupils behind after lessons to talk to them (but I am never alone behind closed doors with any pupil!)
2.
3.
4.
5.
6.
7.
8.
9.
10.

◆ ACTIVITY 3.6 ◆◆◆

It is important to match the sanctions you use to the rules that are broken and to decide whether you are using sanctions effectively.

For this Activity, write down the *five* most frequently broken rules in your classroom. Underneath each one, write down what you actually do first of all to stop the misdemeanor and then to make sure that it doesn't happen again.

At the same time, decide how successful your actions are. If what you do stops the rule being broken most of the time, write 1. If it hardly ever works, write 3. If it works about 50% of the time, write 2. This example might help you.

Rule broken: Pupils rushing into the classroom rather than walking in quietly.

Sanction used: Make pupils go back out and come in quietly. If it happens again, keep them in at break time and make them practise coming into the classroom quietly.

Success rate: 50%, so for this example I would have written 2.

If, when you have finished this Activity, you find that you have frequently written 3, you need to reconsider how you approach rule breaking and decide what changes you need to make to the sanctions you use.

1. *Rule broken*:	
Sanction used:	
Success rate:	

2. *Rule broken:*

Sanction used:

Success rate:

3. *Rule broken:*

Sanction used:

Success rate:

4. *Rule broken:*

Sanction used:

Success rate:

5. *Rule broken:*

Sanction used:

Success rate:

◆ ACTIVITY 3.7 ◆◆◆

In these final Activities, let's try a quiz format which allows you to reflect on your classroom behaviour.

Read each statement or question and grade yourself by ticking the appropriate box:

    A ... You behave like this most of the time
    B ... You behave in this way part of the time
    C ... You hardly ever or never behave in this way

Classroom Behaviour

	A	B	C
1. I use inconsistent sanctions and punishments.			
2. I expect certain of my pupils to behave badly.			
3. I avoid having favourites amongst my pupils.			
4. I often make negative comments in public about my pupils.			
5. I care about and always try to trust my pupils.			
6. I assume that most of my pupils will behave well most of the time.			
7. When my pupils don't want to work and won't settle down to the task in hand, I assume that it is impossible to provide the right conditions.			
8. I always try to avoid confrontations with the pupils I teach.			
9. I tend to give preferential treatment to pupils who conform.			
10. I try to avoid contact with pupils outside the classroom.			
11. I assume that everyone wants to work and if they don't, the conditions, rather than the pupils, are at fault.			

12. When I am teaching, I set unrealistic ultimatums and deadlines.			
13. I rarely make any kind of negative comment about the pupils I teach.			
14. When I do punish pupils, I always give them the chance to tell their side of the story.			
15. I quite enjoy pupils' company outside the classroom.			
16. I believe that discipline is a battle of wills that I have to win.			
17. I am unable to defuse difficult situations.			

◆ ACTIVITY 3.8 ◆◆◆

If you have thought carefully about *Activity 3.7* and have honestly ticked the most appropriate box, you should have found out something quite significant about your classroom management and how you behave when you are teaching. There are many ways of analysing your answers, but let's choose the simplest.

If you have ticked mostly As for these numbers, you are probably a PROVOCA-TIVE teacher:

   1, 2, 4, 7, 9, 10, 12, 16, 17.

If you behave in this kind of way, you will probably PROVOKE and encourage the kind of behaviour you wish to avoid.

If you have ticked mostly As for these numbers, you are what is known as an INSULATING teacher:

   3, 5, 6, 8, 11, 13, 14, 15.

If you behave in this way, you will INSULATE yourself from the kind of deviant behaviour you want to avoid. If you can be or, in fact, are a teacher who falls into the second category, you are more likely to be effective.

Look at your chart in *Activity 3.7* again and choose three aspects of your behaviour that you know you must change. Write these aspects down together with the appropriate responses to the questions that follow.

1. *Behaviour to change*:

Why do you need to change this behaviour?

How will you change it?

2. *Behaviour to change*:

Why do you need to change this behaviour?

How will you change it?

3. *Behaviour to change*:

Why do you need to change this behaviour?

How will you change it?

Charting Deviant Behaviour

Obviously, the more effective you are as a teacher, the fewer discipline problems you will have in the classroom. *But* it needs to be made very, very clear that *every teacher* will have pupils in their classes who cause problems, are disruptive and behave in a deviant way.

The Units so far have emphasised and concentrated on your classroom management skills and your behaviour with your pupils when you are teaching. This one examines the pupils you teach and assumes that the more you know about them and can find out about why they behave in certain ways, the better your chances are of finding ways to improve their behaviour.

◆ ACTIVITY 4.1 ◆◆◆

First of all, think again of one of your pupils whom you find difficult and who causes you problems when you are teaching.

The *Pupil Behaviour Chart* has two sides. There is a POSITIVE side because I am assuming that even the most difficult pupil will have something positive that can be built on and there is a NEGATIVE side because the pupils you are thinking about will be exhibiting a lot of negative behaviour.

Think of your pupil and complete the chart by ticking the appropriate boxes, e.g. looking at the first three items, if the pupil does attend school regularly, tick the +2 column; if you feel s/he is unhappy, tick the -2 column and if you have never really heard her/him say anything about feeling unwell tick the 0 column, and so on until you have completed the whole chart.

In this way you should be able to build up a positive/negative profile of the pupil you feel is causing you problems. This will, hopefully, help you to build on the positive and, by identifying negative aspects, it might suggest those areas where you need to find the underlying causes of the negative behaviour.

Pupil Behaviour Chart

Positive pattern of behaviour	+2	+1	0	-1	-2	Negative patterns of behaviour
Attends school						Misses school
Is happy in school						Is unhappy in school
Has no physical complaints						Complains of aches and pains
Is confident						Lacks confidence
Responds well to discipline						Responds badly to discipline
Parents support the school						Parents don't support the school
Arrives punctually at school						Arrives late for school
Is helpful to others						Is unhelpful to others
Can work and play independently						Finds being independent difficult
Responds well to praise						Responds badly to praise
Behaves well outside class						Behaves badly outside class
Is on-task in class						Is off-task in class
Can remain in seat						Is restless and often out of seat
Is relaxed when on-task						Is irritable and fidgets when on-task
Respects peers						Does not respect peers
Respects others' property						Abuses others' property

Has good concentration						Has poor concentration
Has self-control						Lacks self-control
Moves from task to task easily						Disturbs others between tasks
Settles down quickly						Takes too long to settle
Copes with changes						Cannot cope well with change
Usually asks for help						Waits for help to be provided
Likes to complete tasks						Does not bother to complete tasks
Follows teacher's instructions						Disobeys teacher
Is co-operative with teacher						Is unco-operative with teacher
Can talk positively with teacher						Makes negative remarks to teacher
Is fair to peers						Is unfair to peers
Communicates well with peers						Is uncommunicative with peers
Is not aggressive with peers						Fights peers
Is popular with peers						Is disliked by peers
Is interested in others						Is only interested in self
Is not a bully						Is a bully
Has one or more friends						Has few or no friends
Joins in playground games						Plays alone

◆ **ACTIVITY 4.2** ◆◆◆

Activity 4.1 should have identified several general areas of negative behaviour. Choose the *four* that cause you the most problems, write them down and spend some time completing the boxes below each one.

1. *Negative behaviour*:
What does the pupil you have in mind actually do?
Can you think what triggers this kind of negative behaviour?
What do you do to stop the behaviour or change it to a more positive way of acting?
Does it work? If it does, why does it? If it doesn't, why doesn't it?

2. *Negative behaviour*:
What does the pupil you have in mind actually do?
Can you think what triggers this kind of negative behaviour?

What do you do to stop the behaviour or change it to a more positive way of acting?

Does it work? If it does, why does it? If it doesn't, why doesn't it?

3. *Negative behaviour*:

What does the pupil you have in mind actually do?

Can you think what triggers this kind of negative behaviour?

What do you do to stop the behaviour or change it to a more positive way of acting?

Does it work? If it does, why does it? If it doesn't, why doesn't it?

4. *Negative behaviour*:

What does the pupil you have in mind actually do?

Can you think what triggers this kind of negative behaviour?

What do you do to stop the behaviour or change it to a more positive way of acting?
Does it work? If it does, why does it? If it doesn't, why doesn't it?

◆ **ACTIVITY 4.3** ◆◆◆

We can follow on from the previous Activity by becoming more specific about pupils whose behaviour is frequently irritating or even exceptionally disruptive. Such pupils are time-consuming, increase your stress levels and often make teaching and learning for the majority quite difficult. The more you know about such pupils, the easier it will be to identify ways of helping them.

Think of the same pupil as in the previous two Activities. This time you need to break down some of the general negative areas into more specific behaviour patterns. We shall look at eleven of these.

Tick the appropriate box in each of the eleven areas.

1. Classroom behaviour

Accepts normal discipline	
Needs disciplining occasionally	
Challenges authority and is openly resentful and defiant	

2. Consistency of behaviour

Is well behaved nearly all the time	
Behaves variably	
Is badly behaved almost all the time	

3. Application

Gets on with work steadily	
Works most of the time	
Is restless, distracts others and daydreams	

4. Quality of work in relation to ability

Is commensurate	
Is commensurate at least half the time	
Rarely works to appropriate level	

5. Self-esteem

Is assured, cheerful and positive	
Is generally content with life	
Is negative, gloomy and dissatisfied	

6. Relationship with peers

Has got friends and is generally liked	
Changes friends frequently but is seldom alone	
Hardly interacts with anyone	

7. Relationship with teachers

Is friendly and co-operative	
Relates well much of the time	
Ignores, rejects and is openly hostile	

8. Relationship with ancillary staff

Is friendly and co-operative	
Relates well much of the time	
Ignores, rejects and is openly hostile	

9. Behaviour out of class

Conforms	
Sometimes needs the intervention of authority	
Openly flouts most rules	

10. Response to reproof

Apologises and amends behaviour	
Sometimes needs telling twice	
Rejects or openly disregards admonition	

11. Emotional control

Controls feelings quickly	
Sometimes takes a while to recover equilibrium	
Is unable to suppress strong emotional responses	

Recovering equilibrium.

◆ ACTIVITY 4.4 ◆◆◆

So far, previous Activities have moved from the general towards the more specific identification of the kinds of problems that are caused by a pupil's deviant behaviour. The idea has been that the more you know about the kinds of behaviour that cause problems the easier it will become to decide what course of action to take.

Here is the final identification chart which should, if you think about the same pupil as in previous Activities, provide you with a comprehensive profile of the kinds of deviant behaviour that occur in every classroom at some time or another.

Think of the pupil and if s/he behaves in any of the ways listed, tick those boxes.

Checklist of Behavioural Problems

Moodiness	
Irritability	
Anxiety	
Fear	
Stuttering	
Nervous twitches	
Seeming miserable	
Fussing with trivial complaints	
Vulnerable and the victim of bullying	
Frequent tears	
Immature play with other pupils	
Social isolation	
Excessive quietness	
Talk of suicide	
Attention seeking	
Aggressive attitude	
Hitting other pupils	

Self-mutilation	
Severe tempers	
Cheekiness	
Frequent silliness	
Over-activity	
Truancy	
Frequent absences with poor excuses	
Stealing	
Destructiveness	
Bullying	
Getting others into trouble	
Abuse of drugs, alcohol or glue	
Preoccupation with pornography	

◆   **ACTIVITY 4.5**   ◆◆◆

Activity 4.1 examined both the positive and negative aspects of pupil behaviour and these were followed up in more detail in *Activity 4.3*. It is important not just to view difficult pupils in a negative light. You can say something positive about nearly every pupil you teach. But, obviously, if we are trying to chart deviant behaviour and work out strategies to prevent it happening, we have to be aware, in as much detail as possible, of the kinds of disruptive behaviour to expect and the kinds of problems faced by deviant pupils.

In *Activity 4.2*, you were asked to identify four areas of difficult behaviour and to suggest, for each one, what caused it and how you would deal with it. If you want to use the same four areas again you can, but it would help if you could re-read some of your responses and try to create a more complex picture of the pupil you have been thinking about. Whilst it is always going to be important to recognise and praise the positive, it is the bad behaviour that will cause you the most problems.

For example, your pupil might challenge you openly, restlessly move about the classroom, rarely work to her/his appropriate level and be openly hostile to ancillary staff. At the same time, s/he could be the victim of bullying, stutter and be very immature … I am sure you would agree, quite a complex profile.

But, at the end of the day, if such pupils are in your classroom, causing you problems, you have to develop strategies to deal with the immediate difficulty in the short term and begin to solve the whole of the problem in the long term.

So think again of *four* problems caused by a pupil, or pupils in your classroom that are very difficult to deal with. Write them down in the spaces below.

1.
2.
3.
4.

❖

◆ ACTIVITY 4.6 ◆◆◆

It is important to consider ways of stopping the deviant and disruptive behaviour immediately while at the same time seeing the problem as a longer-term issue. You must have thought about this in *Activity 4.2* and in a more generalised way in previous Units. In this Activity, a specified list of possible actions you could take is given.

Read through the list and, for each suggestion, decide whether you could use it to try to solve one or more of your four problems from *Activity 4.5*. If you could, place a tick in the relevant boxes, e.g. if you think that praising desirable behaviour could be used to solve your first and third problems, put a tick in boxes 1 and 3 for that action.

Checklist of Possible Action

	1	2	3	4
1. Overlook and ignore the undesirable behaviour				
2. Remind pupil that you disapprove				
3. Discuss the problem with her/him				
4. Reprimand the pupil privately				
5. Discipline the pupil in front of the group				
6. Alter the seating arrangements in the room				
7. Reorganise the class by regrouping pupils				
8. Check that there is a match between the pupil's ability and the work that is set				
9. Look at, and read, the pupil's records				
10. Check whether the pupil is well (medically)				
11. Check for any changes in the pupil's home circumstances				
12. Keep the pupil in at break				
13. Give the pupil extra work to do				
14. Deprive the pupil of privileges				
15. Send the pupil out of the room				
16. Send the pupil to another teacher				
17. Arrange a detention				
18. Send the pupil to the Head/Deputy/Head of Department				

19. Use the pupil's first name more frequently				
20. Smile at the pupil more frequently				
21. Notice the pupil more often				
22. Praise desirable behaviour				
23. Praise small improvements in her/his work				
24. Avoid showing public disapproval of the pupil's work or behaviour				
25. Help the pupil with work/self-organisation/ study skills, etc.				
26. With the pupil, negotiate and sign a contract for better pupil behaviour				
27. Increase friendly contacts with the pupil				
28. Explain the pupil's difficulty to the class				
29. Encourage peers to include the pupil in groups				
30. Encourage peers to ignore disruptive behaviour				
31. Enhance the pupil's status by giving her/him desirable jobs				

◆ **ACTIVITY 4.7** ◆◆◆

Activity 4.6 may have suggested actions that you have not considered before. As a final Activity, I want you to think about the consequences of using these sanctions.

What you have to do is answer a series of questions. There are spaces below each one for your responses.

1. What do you think might happen if you constantly use numbers 12–18?

2. Will they help to solve any of your problems?

3. When, and under what circumstances, do these kinds of sanctions work?

4. What is likely to happen in your classroom if you mostly use number 19 onwards?

5. Will they help the pupils who disrupt because of their deviant behaviour?

6. Is there sometimes the need for 'pure' punishment?

7. If there is, under what circumstances would you punish your pupils?

Teacher/Pupil Relationships

You can influence the atmosphere of your classroom by relating to your pupils in certain ways. All the Units so far have openly, or by implication, suggested effective ways for teachers to behave. This short Unit takes this a stage further by suggesting how you can influence the success of teaching and learning. This is important because good classroom management and constructive teaching are based on good relationships, high self-esteem amongst pupils and a sense of working together within a community. A successful teacher always establishes a management structure in which there is a working consensus with widely accepted rules about such things as noise levels, how pupils answer questions and how they move around the room. This Unit suggests how this 'working consensus' is established, so that pupils see the classroom as the place to work hard and sensibly.

Each of the Activities asks some questions and space is provided for your answers.

◆ ACTIVITY 5.1 ◆◆◆

In your relationships with your pupils you must be careful not to use UNFAIR SANCTIONS. This usually happens when you lose control.

1. When did you last lose your temper? Why did it happen? Did your pupils gain anything from it?

2. When did you last do something in your classroom that the majority of pupils felt was unfair? What kind of classroom atmosphere resulted from it?

❖

◆ **ACTIVITY 5.2** ◆ ◆ ◆

Your relationships with your pupils will improve and remain good if you use
ACCEPTED ROUTINE SANCTIONS. If pupils routinely misbehave, e.g. talk out
of turn, they will accept that they should be routinely reprimanded.

---

1. What kinds of routine reprimands do you use that work and yet don't
   threaten the pupils too much? Make a list.

---

2. Do any of your pupils resent these kinds of sanctions? If they do, why do
   they?

An accepted routine sanction.

◆ **ACTIVITY 5.3** ◆ ◆ ◆

Much of the behaviour in your classroom and many of the activities will depend on everyone conforming to certain conventions and agreements. There will, however, be ROUTINE MISBEHAVIOUR which should be accepted by everyone as part of pupils' growing up. Within reasons, it is fairly normal behaviour. Examples include occasionally talking too loudly, inappropriate laughter and working too slowly.

---

1. What sort of routine misbehaviour do you expect and 'allow' in your classroom?

---

2. What do you do if it becomes more than routine?

◆ **ACTIVITY 5.4** ◆ ◆ ◆

There is, unfortunately, classroom behaviour which, as we discussed in *Unit 4*, is DEVIANT, DISRUPTIVE and capable of destroying teacher/pupil relationships.

---

1. How does this kind of behaviour destroy pupil/teacher relationships?

---

2. What action could you take that would minimise this damage to relationships?

◆ ACTIVITY 5.5 ◆◆◆

The following four short Activities suggest not only how you could build up better teacher/pupil relationships, but how you could increase your pupils' self-esteem. This is extremely important because, as I have suggested before, many pupils who cause problems and threaten classroom relationships suffer from low self-esteem.

If a pupil behaves badly, you are certainly right to be shocked and disappointed with her/him. *But* try and avoid telling the pupil that s/he is bad. Concentrate on punishing the act rather than the person.

How would you do this? Write down an example, such as bullying, swearing in the classroom or shouting out a sexist comment, and write down how you would deal with it.

◆ ACTIVITY 5.6 ◆◆◆

Many pupils who are likely to challenge your authority over and above routine misbehaviour are likely to feel threatened. If it is possible, you should try to minimise the threat of failure by saying before a task:

'This might be quite hard but I know you'll do your best … ' or 'Try not to worry if this is too difficult …'

> Write down any situations where you feel you might use this technique to build up a pupil's self-esteem and improve your relationship with her/him. At the same time, write down what you might say.

◆ ACTIVITY 5.7 ◆◆◆

Those pupils, whom you need to support by preventing them from failing, will probably have a short attention span and may well need rapid feedback during and immediately after activities.

> How would you know when to intervene and offer support?
>
>
> What kind of support would you offer and what would you say?

◆ **ACTIVITY 5.8** ◆◆◆

Finally, there is the need to realise that relationships within a classroom cannot and will not be built up and improved by a teacher who has her/his own space within the classroom – usually a desk – and spends much of the time within that space.

An effective teacher is constantly on the move in and out of the desks and round and round the classroom and constantly uses both verbal and non-verbal signals, interventions and support.

Think about a lesson you will be teaching shortly and draw a plan of the classroom in the space below. If the room is the same and you have space on the plan you drew in earlier Activities, use that one.

Either during the lesson or immediately after it, add to the plan your route around the classroom. Mark who you speak to in a supportive way. (This will help to build up classroom relationships.) Mark who you speak to in a negative way.

At the end of the lesson, do you feel you were more positive than negative? Did you miss anyone out? Did you speak to everyone? Did you move everywhere?

Case Studies and Action Plans

This book is concerned with managing your classroom successfully, so that teaching and learning take place effectively. By looking at teaching styles, different aspects of managing a busy classroom, how teachers behave with their pupils and the kinds of deviant behaviour that disrupt the best run classrooms, there is bound to be some overlap of content, ideas and methods. After all, teaching styles are all about managing the teaching of a lesson and dealing with disruptive behaviour. At the same time, how you behave with your pupils will be largely determined by the teaching style you adopt and will influence the kind of relationships that are built up between you and your pupils. This, in turn, will influence how your pupils behave and how you enforce sanctions and rules … etc. etc.

With this in mind, this Unit is in two parts.

Activity 6.1 contains some Case Studies which are as realistic as possible.

Activity 6.2 is a series of Action Plans for the future. They relate to specific areas of the book which you should re-read before completing each action plan.

Do remember that if you have reflected honestly on your classroom management and teaching skills, you should find that these final Activities will help you to improve your practice. Certainly use the charts in *Unit 4* to help you with any disruptive pupils in the future.

Those of you who are curriculum co-ordinators or hold senior positions may like to use some of the suggestions in the Activities with colleagues.

◆ ACTIVITY 6.1 ◆◆◆

Read the case studies and respond to the questions that are asked about them. What you write in the spaces will depend on what you have discovered about your teaching and management in all the Units of this book. In other words, how you deal with the problem described in the case study will depend on a wide range of overlapping skills and ideas.

Case study 1

Shelia is a physically small, immature pupil with few friends. Her clothes suggest that she is from a relatively poor background. In the classroom, she does not produce much work. she has some special needs in that her writing is poorly formed and she finds some aspects of Maths difficult, but when you teach her you receive no extra support. Rather than finish what she has started, she seeks attention by losing pens and pencils, accusing other pupils of taking them and getting out of her seat to wander round the room. She is happiest in the classroom when she is given a job to do which involves running errands or tidying the room. Outside the classroom, she is always in the wrong place at the wrong time and is rude and disruptive with ancillary staff. This is getting worse and the kind of insolent behaviour she uses with lunchtime supervisors is now being turned on you. Her mother hardly ever comes to school and has, in the past, had to be persuaded to come to open days.

What can you do to improve Sheila's attitude to work?
What can you do to improve her self-esteem?
What will you be able to do to help her remain on-task for longer?
How can you improve her behaviour and attitude outside the classroom?

Case study 2

Jake is large, loud, intolerant and verbally and physically violent towards his peers. Consequently, no one likes him and yet he is desperately trying to belong to a friendship group. His parents feel that he is a wonderful, extremely clever boy and have brought him up to believe that the world is a tough place and, therefore, he needs to be better, smarter and stronger than everyone else. He has few social graces, fewer manners and a reputation throughout the school of being a trouble maker. Despite the fact that his parents think he is clever, he is not. In fact, he borders on needing some input from the school's Special Needs Co-ordinator. The last time this was raised with his parents, his father became abusive. Jake is becoming more and more difficult. He has recently sworn at a teacher and hit a pupil so hard that there were parental complaints. It is suspected that there are problems at home. Last week he came to school with facial bruising.

First of all, what sanctions could you use to stop Jake behaving badly in the classroom?
This seems to be a whole school issue. What should the school do to improve Jake's attitude and behaviour?
What teaching styles might work best with a pupil like Jake?
Is there anything you could do to help to improve his class work?

Case study 3

Mark is a bully. He has been caught once demanding money from younger pupils. Since then, he and his group of followers have been suspected of doing several things to other pupils but never caught. In the classroom, Mark has few friends, finds it very difficult to work in a group and is largely avoided by his peers because of his moodiness and random violence. He is an able pupil with a lot of potential, but he will not admit that he knows anything, doesn't answer questions and does the minimum amount of work. When disciplined, he sulks and doesn't talk or runs away from school. All his friends are younger and have learning difficulties. Because of this he finds it easy to dominate them.

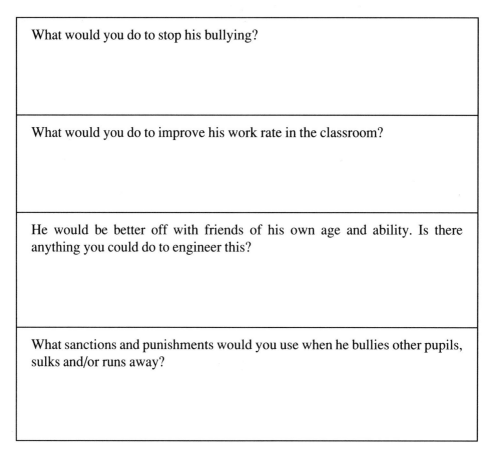

What would you do to stop his bullying?

What would you do to improve his work rate in the classroom?

He would be better off with friends of his own age and ability. Is there anything you could do to engineer this?

What sanctions and punishments would you use when he bullies other pupils, sulks and/or runs away?

If you find these Case Studies difficult, it might help if you discuss you responses with a trusted colleague.

◆ ACTIVITY 6.2 ◆◆◆

Rather than examining both positive and negative issues, all the Action Plans concentrate on those styles, skills and classroom management techniques that need improving.

Action Plan 1

Which kinds of classroom behaviour do you need to be able to model more effectively and how will you go about doing it?
1.   2.   3.   4.   5.
When you are being consistent, firm and fair, what do you need to do to be more effective?
1.   2.   3.   4.   5.
Pupils need praise. How could you be better at praising your pupils?
1.   2.   3.   4.   5.

Action Plan 2

Which particular teaching styles from *Activity 1.6* and *Activity 2.5* do you need to improve? List five of them and say what you are going to do to be more successful.

1.

2.

3.

4.

5.

Action Plan 3

Which non-verbal cues from *Activity 1.9* do you need to improve? How are you going to use them more effectively?

1.

2.

3.

4.

5.

Action Plan 4

Lesson planning is extremely important.

I am going to improve my planning by doing the following:
1.
2.
3.
4.
5.

Lesson planning.

Action Plan 5

Every classroom needs to have effective rules.

I intend introducing and implementing the following new rules:
1.
2.
3.
4.
I intend using the following established rules more effectively:
1.
2.
3.
4.

Action Plan 6

When trying to deal with disruptive and deviant behaviour it is important to know as much about your pupils as possible.

In future I am going to try and find out the following:
1.
2.
3.
4.
5.

Action Plan 7

Disruptive behaviour is always difficult to deal with but some kinds are more difficult than others.

I find the following kinds of misbehaviour the most difficult to deal with:
1.
2.
3.
4.
5.

Action Plan 8

Because I find it difficult to deal with some kinds of disruptions, I am going either to start using the following sanctions or I am going to improve how I use them:
1.
2.
3.
4.
5.

And that, as they say, is that. I hope this book has been useful and thought provoking. Do keep thinking about your teaching and reflecting on both your successful and less successful lessons.

Further Reading

Montgomery, D., *Managing Behaviour Problems* (London, Hodder and Stoughton, 1989)

Moon, B. and Shelton Mayes, A. (eds.), *Teaching and Learning in the Secondary School* (London, Routledge, 1994)

Pollard, A. and Tann, S., *Reflective Teaching in the Primary School: A Handbook for the Classroom* (London, Cassell, 1993)

Smith, R., *The Effective School, Vols. 1 and 2* (Lancaster, Framework Press, 1990)

Smith, R., 'Elusive ethos', *Managing Schools Today*, 2: 6 (1993)

Smith, R., *Managing Pupil Behaviour in School and Classroom: In-house Training Materials for Teachers* (Lancaster, Framework Press, 1993)